A Layman's Guide to the INERRANCY DEBATE

Richard P. Belcher

MOODY PRESS
CHICAGO

ISBN: 0-8024-2379-5

Printed in the United States of America

Contents

Foreword

Our world is a world of uncertainty, catastrophic upheaval, and destitution. People once groped in the darkness after answers, but now a mood of despair has settled over humanity, which underlines the simple fact that many people have given up on finding answers to life's perplexing dilemmas.

What an ineffable joy it is for me to see this succinct treatise from the hand of my dear professor friend Richard Belcher, which reaffirms the central plank in the platform of evangelical Christianity, namely, that God has spoken a sure word in time and history. The characteristic uncertainty of theological proclamation in our day seems to have crippled the great churches and denominations of America. That there is yet hope and a new day ahead can be observed clearly in the affirmations of professor Belcher's essays.

Read the essays carefully and reflect on their significance because they reaffirm the full inerrancy and infallibility of the blessed Book that the Holy Spirit gave through the prophets and the apostles. You will find your soul moved with thanksgiving to God who has provided us so wonderfully with a sure word and a bright light in a dark day.

W. A. CRISWELL

Introduction

With love for all and with deep respect for those with whom I differ, I set forth my thoughts in these essays on the current controversy over the nature of Scripture. Before so doing, I wish to clarify several points.

First, this is not a systematic presentation of the doctrine of Scripture. These essays have been written from the thoughts that have emerged from the heat of debate on the various questions surrounding the issue of inerrancy. Each essay stands independent of the others, but each relates to the same issue and problem.

Second, these essays do not claim to settle the

issue. Rather, an attempt is made to deal with only some (not all) of the key points of the discussion concerning the nature of Scripture. Other questions still remain, and others will emerge as the debate continues. These essays, however, deal with some of the problems I have encountered in my reading and discussion of the overall controversy.

Third, I am not involved in any campaign against any denomination or denominations. The problem of the nature of Scripture cuts across denominational lines. Denominational books or their publishing houses are not a target of my pen or position. The issues must remain the concern.

Last, these essays have not been written primarily for the scholars involved in the controversy. The inerrancy issue is one of the most confusing and perplexing for the lay person to seek to understand. I hope these essays have been written so that the issue and the answers to crucial questions might be seen by the laity. For many years I have carried a burden that the complex issues of theology, which are so often discussed in ivory tower terminology, might be made clear to the layman who desires and needs to understand.

It is hoped the reader will remember these introductory remarks as he reads each essay. How difficult it is to deal with controversial subjects without appearing controversial in attitude. May the subject of discussion and my attitude come through with clarity.

1

Is the Doctrine of Verbal Inspiration Dead?

It is commonly assumed in scholarly circles, even among many evangelicals, that the doctrine of verbal inspiration of Scripture is dead. However, the corpse awaits burial, because many of the laity and untrained pastors still hold tenaciously to it and refuse to admit what the scholars claim. The doctors of theology have examined the body, read the pulse, assessed the life signs, and concluded (not always sadly) that verbal inspiration choked on the claim of inerrancy and the too rigid concept of mechanical dictation. The laity must now be reeducated so that it will know and agree with what the scholars already know to be a certainty. Care must be taken to work slowly and inconspicuously at that task lest the uneducated and uninformed be sent into shock over the truth of their beloved's passing. The news, however, must be filtered to them through the schools and publishing houses and from more enlightened pulpits. In time the majority will agree with the decree of the scholars that the concept of verbal inspiration is dead and has given way to a more excellent concept.

For several years now the process of reeducation has been descending upon us. Many persons have been convinced by the scholars; others feel it really makes no difference; another large group is puzzled by it all. A few understand the problem and its implications.

Before one yields to the conclusion of the scholars, he needs to ask some questions. On what grounds have the theologians come to their conclusions? Are they correct in their diagnosis? Are they fair in their judgments? Have they examined the right body? Is verbal inspiration really dead?

This essay will deal with those questions and their overall relation to the main question concerning the supposed death of the doctrine of verbal inspiration. First, we shall look at a common line of argument against verbal inspiration. Second, we shall examine the view commonly substituted in place of verbal inspiration. Third, we shall give an example from a present-day writer of a line of argument that is thought to destroy verbal inspiration. Last, we shall critique that line of argument to determine if its conclusion is correct concerning the "death" of verbal inspiration.

A Line of Argument against the Doctrine of Verbal Inspiration

A common line of argumentation against the doctrine of verbal inspiration bears a two-pronged attack. The first prong says that verbal inspiration equals mechanical dictation. The second prong indicates that the infallibility and inerrancy claimed by verbal inspiration cannot exist because of obvious errors in the text of Scripture. On the foundation of these two arguments it is concluded that verbal inspiration is dead. This conclusion opens the door for a substitute, more liberal view of the Bible and its inspiration. This view says that the "truth" of Scripture is inspired, but not the individual words. The dynamic view, as it is sometimes called, solves the problems left by mechanical dictation by allowing for a difference in the styles and vocabularies of the various biblical writers. The claim is made that the dynamic view also gives a proper balance between the divine and the human in the revelational encounter. Furthermore, the dynamic view is said to solve the problem of errors in the Bible by acknowledging them, while still safeguarding the truth of the Bible.

AN EXAMPLE OF SUCH LINE OF ARGUMENT

Such a process of argumentation is repeated constantly in classrooms, discussions, and writings. An example is offered from an essay by James Flamming in a recent book.[1] Flamming relates an experience he encountered while teaching Genesis in a Sunday school class. One of his pupils had come across what Flamming calls a difference in the accounts of creation in Genesis 1:1—2:3 and 2:4-25. When the student questioned him about the two supposedly different accounts, Flamming replied that the writing of Genesis 1-11 was transmitted orally until the time of David and Solomon, when those stories finally were written down. The student then protested by saying, "I have always thought it was written by God who just dictated to men what he wanted them to say."[2] After further discussion between the teacher and student, the teacher asked, "But has the Spirit of God assumed the stance of a dictator, dictating what he wants said? Or does he take the personal stance of mutual faith and trust working within the greatness and weakness of human personalities?"[3] The teacher continued a few sentences later by saying, "It would seem a book dictated by one person would bear the same similarities in vocabu-

1. James Flamming, "Could God Trust Human Hands?" in *Is the Bible a Human Book?*, ed. Joseph Green and Wayne E. Ward (Nashville: Broadman, 1970), pp. 9-18.
2. Ibid., p. 9.
3. Ibid., pp. 9-10.

lary, style, environmental background, and emphases."[4]

At this point in Flamming's discussion, prong one of the attack is finished. The student in the Sunday school class has presented a view of mechanical dictation. The teacher has shown its absurdity by noting the differences of style, vocabulary, and environmental background of the various Bible writers. Though Flamming does not say in specific words that verbal inspiration equals mechanical dictation, the total essay leads one to that conclusion. He does not mention any other possible view of inspiration as he presents his view against mechanical dictation. If he is aware that many persons hold to the doctrine of verbal inspiration but deny that mechanical dictation is a proper representation of that doctrine, he does not mention it. And if he *is* aware of this position on verbal inspiration, then he has been guilty of constructing a straw man for the purpose of easily defeating the orthodox concept of verbal inspiration. One must assume that, for Flamming, verbal inspiration equals mechanical dictation. Mechanical dictation falls very easily to the simple noting of differing styles and vocabularies in the different books of the Bible.

The second prong of attack then begins. Flamming now recognizes supposed errors in the Bible. These alleged errors destroy any possibility, in his thinking, for biblical inerrancy and infallibility.

4. Ibid., p. 10.

All of the supposed errors that Flamming discusses cannot be presented here, but several will be mentioned as examples.

Flamming says that Mark is in error when he joins a quotation from Malachi with one from Isaiah (Mark 1:2-3) and then attributes the quotation to Isaiah.[5] Again, Mark is supposedly mistaken when he names Abiathar as the high priest when it was really Abiathar's father Ahimelech (1 Samuel 21:1-6 and Mark 2:23-28).[6] Flamming contends that Mark was just too anxious to get his message across and was not careful in writing. He made the error of an impatient man of action. Seeking to comfort hearts that might tremble at the thought of errors in Scripture, Flamming says, "If God could use Mark with sixth grade grammar, and an occasional misquote from the Old Testament, maybe he can use me too!"[7]

The second prong of argumentation is now complete. The errors are pieces of humanity throughout Scripture, and they make inerrancy impossible.[8] The implication is that verbal inspiration is impossible. Flamming says, "The picture we seem to get is not that God dictated the materials. Rather, in spite of human weakness, God seems to trust man to sense and record the major redemp-

---

5. Ibid., pp. 10-11.
6. Ibid., p. 11.
7. Ibid.
8. Ibid.
9. Ibid., p. 13.

tive themes."[9]

Flamming's next step is to offer an alternate view concerning inspiration, a view that does not present the problems encountered in mechanical dictation. Such a view must allow for the different styles and vocabularies of the biblical writers, allow for the errors that Flamming is convinced exist, and properly balance the human and divine in the process of revelation. Flamming presents the dynamic view of inspiration as the substitute for mechanical dictation. The dynamic view says that even though there are errors in the Bible, the doctrinal truth is still present.

Flamming says, "All of these questions summed up and put together do not subtract from the impact of the birth, life, death, and resurrection of our Lord Jesus Christ."[10] That is to say, the errors of the Bible and other problems do not negate the truth of the birth, life, death, and resurrection of Christ. Although the Bible has errors in it, it still bears infallible doctrinal truth.

Not only does a dynamic view solve the problem of errors and yet preserve the truth, it also allows for different styles and vocabularies among the biblical writers, and supposedly balances the divine and human aspects in the process of biblical revelation.

A CRITIQUE OF THE ARGUMENT

The next portion of this essay will examine sev-

10. Ibid., p. 12.

eral weaknesses in Flamming's line of reasoning against verbal inspiration.

First, this method of argument has examined the wrong corpse. The whole case is built on the presupposition that verbal inspiration equals mechanical dictation. When the wrong body (mechanical dictation) is examined, it is easily seen to have a serious ailment—the problem of differing styles and vocabularies in the Bible. On the other hand, when the right body (the proper understanding of verbal inspiration) is examined, there is no such problem. In simple words, verbal inspiration does not equal mechanical dictation. Mechanical dictation is a straw man set up by the opponents of verbal inspiration so that they may easily defeat the doctrine of verbal inspiration.

But there are similarities between verbal inspiration and mechanical dictation. Both see God as the author of Scripture. Both acknowledge man as the agent involved in inspiration. Both agree that the result is a perfect and infallible text in the original manuscripts. Both hold that the words and truth of Scripture are inerrant. On the basis of those similarities, many have concluded that the two are equal. To reach such a conclusion demonstrates a failure to distinguish precisely one's categories of thought. It shows also an unawareness of the scholars who have set forth carefully a proper view of verbal inspiration.

The crucial difference between the two is on the matter of balance between the human and divine.

Mechanical dictation overbalances in the direction of the divine. A perfect book is the result, but at the expense of man's full involvement. The varying vocabularies and styles of the writers are bypassed—God simply used the writers as passive tools, as a man would use a typewriter. However, a proper understanding of verbal inspiration fully balances the human and the divine, and yet produces a perfect text as the result. God, by His full power, used man in his full powers and thereby guaranteed a reliable text.

Second, the theologians have erred in their judgment when they conclude that the Bible is full of errors. There are problems because of our lack of knowledge, but this does not give one the right to jump to the conclusion that such gaps in knowledge are errors. Competent scholars have already answered some of those alleged errors. Other supposed errors are still being considered as more understanding of the problems comes to us. Three of Flamming's supposed errors can be answered easily.

1. Flamming says there are two different accounts of creation in Genesis 1:1—2:3 and 2:4-25. On this basis he implies that one must deny the Mosaic authorship in favor of oral transmission, written much later than Moses' time. But why does one have to conclude that those are two separate and different accounts of creation? Can it not be easily seen that the first is a general account of the activity of God on the various days of

creation, whereas the second gives a detailed account of the creation of man and its accompanying events? Writers use the same method today. First comes a survey, followed by further details in later chapters.

2. Concerning the alleged error of Mark 1:2-3, in which Mark joins two prophetic quotations and attributes the resultant quotation to Isaiah, no less authority than A. T. Robertson says, "But Isaiah is mentioned as the chief of the prophets. It was common to combine quotations from the prophets in *testimonia* and *catenae* (chains of quotations)."[11] Therefore Mark did not err because of impatient action. He was only following a common practice of the day, which caused no one to accuse him of a mistake. It is only someone today, who is unaware of that practice, who would make an accusation of error and challenge the practice.

3. Concerning Mark's supposed error in naming Abiathar as high priest when it was his father Ahimelech (1 Samuel 21:6 and Mark 2:23-28), the Greek text does not tie us to the conclusion that Mark is naming Abiathar high priest. Robertson notes that *epi Abiathar archiereos* is a Greek idiom that means "in the time of Abiathar."[12] This could make the statement a general reference to the times of Abiathar and not to his definite period of service. In the same text Robertson suggests that

11. A. T. Robertson, *Word Pictures in the New Testament,* 6 vols. (Nashville: Broadman, 1930), 1:252.
12. Ibid., 1:273.

it is possible both Ahimelech the father and Abiathar the son bore both names.[13] Or their periods of service might have overlapped. In any case it is a premature and uncertain conclusion to call this an error.

The preceding are only three examples of the many supposed errors cited by the opponents of verbal inspiration. Careful and patient research will bring answers to many other alleged errors in Scripture.

Third, the alternate view (dynamic concept of inspiration) has many weaknesses. Obviously, if a medical diagnosis of a patient is in error, then the prescribed treatment is not likely to fit the patient. The theologians of the day have examined the wrong patient (mechanical dictation) and have prescribed the wrong solution (a dynamic concept).

Having already dealt with the accusation that there are errors in the Bible, we now must address the claim that the dynamic view best balances the human and the divine in the inspiration of Scripture. Admission has been made that the mechanical view does overbalance in the direction of the divine. However, a dynamic concept overbalances in the direction of the human by allowing for errors in the original text. As stated earlier, a true understanding of verbal inspiration sees full divine power employing man's full powers, both

13. Ibid.

working in complete cooperation to produce a perfect text of Scripture. This gives a proper balance between the human and the divine in the inspiration of Scripture.

The following chart, comparing the three views being discussed, will be helpful.

	God the Author	Man the Agent	Result a Perfect Book	Truth Inerrant	Words Inerrant	Balance Between Human and Divine
Mechanical	Yes	Yes	Yes	Yes	Yes	No—an overbalance toward the divine. A perfect book, but at the expense of man's full involvement.
Verbal	Yes	Yes	Yes	Yes	Yes	Yes—a perfect book and a perfect balance. God and man involved, yet no destruction of the truth.
Dynamic	Yes	Yes	No	Yes (claimed)	No	No—an overbalance toward the human because errors are claimed to be in the Bible. God and man involved, but a destruction of the truth.

Conclusion

We have shown one of the common attacks against the doctrine of verbal inspiration. The first part of the agrument seeks to make verbal inspiration equal to mechanical dictation. The second part claims errors in the Bible. On the basis of those arguments, verbal inspiration is considered dead. We are told, however, that we must not mourn because the scholars have shown us a better way, the way of dynamic inspiration. This great cure has rescued the infallible truth of the Bible from the "grave" of verbal inspiration just in time. The task now before the proponents of the dynamic view is the re-education of the masses who still ignorantly sing the praises of verbal inspiration.

The truth of the matter is that the doctrine of verbal inspiration is not dead! The accusation of errors in the text of Scripture does not stand. Supposed errors are based on the judgments of prejudiced minds. For the opponents of verbal inspiration to be the scholars they claim to be, they must abandon their attack on the straw man of mechanical dictation and face the true claims of verbal inspiration. May we orthodox evangelicals resist the efforts of such scholars to re-educate us to the need for a more dynamic concept of inspiration—one that speaks of inerrant truth through erring words.

2

Is Scripture Alone the Essence of Christianity?

In a recent essay, Bernard Ramm raises anew the question of the essence (*Wesen*) of Christianity.[1] The choice, as he presents the situation, is between a theory of biblical inspiration with complete inerrancy and the doctrines relating to the death and resurrection of Christ for our sins. Ramm acknowledges that A. A. Hodge and B. B. Warfield held a strong view of inerrancy, but that they refused to make that view of the Bible the essence of Christianity.[2] The current followers of Warfield and Hodge, according to Ramm, have shifted from that position and are now claiming

1. Bernard Ramm, "Is 'Scripture Along' the Essence of Christianity?" in *Biblical Authority,* ed. Jack Rogers (Waco, Texas: Word, 1977) pp. 109-23.
2. Ibid., p. 111.

the doctrine of Scripture as the essence of Christianity. In discussing this point he says:

> One's doctrine of Scripture has become now the first and most important doctrine, one's theory of the *Wesen* of Christianity, so that all other doctrines have validity now only as they are part of the inerrant Scripture. Thus evangelical teachers, or evangelical schools or evangelical movements, can be judged as to whether or not they are true to the *Wesen* of Christianity by their theory of inspiration. It can be stated even more directly: an evangelical has made a theory of inspiration the *Wesen* of Christianity if he assumes that the most important doctrine in a man's theology, and the most revelatory of the entire range of his theological thought, is his theology of inspiration.[3]

Ramm is to be commended for warning those who hold to the doctrine of biblical inerrancy of a potential misemphasis. Truly the essence of Christian faith and doctrine centers on the person and work of Jesus Christ. Positively, this is the core of the gospel that must be proclaimed to a lost world. This gospel is the power of God unto salvation, not one's view of Scripture. We thank Ramm for this observation and reminder.

However, at several points I must take issue with Ramm. First, who are those "current followers of Warfield and Hodge" who have made inerrancy the essence of Christianity? In his entire article Ramm never identifies those whom he is refuting.

3. Ibid., p. 112.

There is not a single footnote of documentation to be found. The whole argument rests upon the premise that some of the "current followers of Hodge and Warfield" have made Biblical inerrancy the *Wesen* of Christianity. The premise is an assumed one and is never proved in the entire essay. Are those persons that Ramm speaks of scholars, pastors, or lay people? Documentation would allow the reader to judge for himself the truth of Ramm's premise. Lack of documentation raises serious questions concerning his essay. Has he constructed a straw man to enable him to champion his own position over against that of biblical inerrancy?

Second, I would take issue with Ramm for his failure to see a crucial relationship between the doctrine of biblical inerrancy and the *Wesen* of Christianity. The reason many evangelicals are so concerned about upholding the doctrine of inerrancy is not because they wish to make that viewpoint the essence of Christianity, but because they perceive clearly a relationship between inerrancy and the *Wesen*. To many evangelicals, the battle with liberal theology early in this century points out such a relationship and demonstrates the loss of Christianity's *Wesen* when the doctrine of biblical inerrancy is rejected. Honesty and fairness demand one to acknowledge quickly that the battle with old liberalism is past and the situation is quite different today. Nonetheless, that battle provides us with an important lesson. It was no accident that old liberalism came to a denial of the deity, substitutionary death, and resurrection of Jesus Christ. That was the logical outcome of its view of Scripture.

Again, one must note that this is a different day. Those today who deny biblical inerrancy, but at the same time still seek to uphold the doctrines of evangelical Christianity, are not liberals. To say that, however, does not exonerate the evangelical errantists because, in a real sense, the old liberals were more consistent than many modern evangelicals. The liberal theologian denied the inerrancy and authority of Scripture and therefore also denied the doctrinal essence of Christianity.

The modern evangelical viewpoint brings deep concern to other evangelicals who hold to the inerrancy of Scripture—a concern that is not being understood by those who deny inerrancy. Several questions lie at the heart of this concern.

1. Is it consistent to hold to biblical authority and yet deny biblical inerrancy?
2. Will not this viewpoint of denying inerrancy while seeking to uphold biblical authority lead us to greater subjectivity in interpreting the Bible, even to the eventual loss or change of the essential doctrines of Christianity?
3. Can the evangelicals who hold to an errant Bible guarantee that the succeeding generations of their scholars will also hold to the essential doctrines of Christianity?

The problem is that the results of this modern

evangelicalism will not be known or open to judgment for some years to come. And even then judgment may be possible only after the other essential doctrines of Christianity have been discarded. That is not to say that a doctrinal viewpoint is judged on a completely pragmatic basis. Nor is it to say that those holding to biblical inerrancy have some doubt concerning their position, which could be settled by a knowledge of the future. I am saying that those who are certain of biblical inerrancy are being asked by a group of evangelicals to accept that group's view of errancy as a valid position, even when there are still too many unanswered questions regarding its present status and future developments.

Conclusion

I am not arguing for biblical inerrancy as the essence of Christianity. Ramm may accuse inerrancy proponents of that, but he did not prove his case. I acknowledge that the *Wesen* of Christianity centers on the person, work, and salvation of Jesus Christ.

I am seeking to defend biblical inerrancy because of a relationship that I am convinced exists between the doctrine of Scripture and the essence of Christianity.

That conviction does not make the doctrine of inerrancy the essence of Christianity any more than a concern for a clean hospital operating room makes that the essence of surgery.

3

Inerrant Truth Through Errant Words?

A conviction is growing among evangelicals that not all parts, words, or details were without error in the original manuscripts of the Bible. That conviction is not speaking of copies or versions, but of the originals themselves. Adherents of that position are not always in agreement regarding which portions are fully inspired and which are not, nor are they explicit in the full statement of their own convictions. Essentially, the position maintains that it is not necessary to hold to inerrant original manuscripts in order to be sure of the infallibility of the truth. Errant words are supposedly capable of conveying the infallible truth of God.

An example of that viewpoint is described in an essay by Clifton J. Allen.[1] First of all the viewpoint speaks of the truth of Scripture with no mention of the words.

> The Scriptures are indeed inspired ("God-breathed") because their truth is from God and about God.[2]

---

1. Clifton J. Allen, "The Book of the Christian Faith," in *The Broadman Bible Commentary*, ed. Clifton J. Allen et al, 12 vols. (Nashville: Broadman, 1969, 1973), 1:1-14.
2. Ibid., p. 6.

> The truth of the biblical revelation is God-breathed.[3]
>
> Consequently, a dynamic view of inspiration focuses on the truth which has its essence and purpose and authority in Jesus Christ.[4]

In further quotations from Allen it is shown that although that viewpoint holds to the truth of Scripture as trustworthy, it denies the inerrancy of the words and details. He says:

> According to this view, the inspiration of the Bible is much more its completeness and adequacy as the written record of God's self-revelation and as the guide for man in all matters of faith and practice than it is a matter of inerrancy in wording and analogy and certain details about persons and events.[5]
>
> Therefore, a dynamic view of inspiration is not dependent on a mystical, inexplicable, and unverifiable inerrancy in every word of Scripture or on the concept that inspiration can allow no error of fact or substance.[6]

Allen subsequently adopts this viewpoint and says that the Bible contains probable errors of fact and substance in its words and details of persons and events. The Bible is not inerrant or infallible in its original manuscripts, at least not according to the historic usage of *inerrant* and *infallible* in reference to Scripture.

The surprise is that Allen still used the word

---

3. Ibid., p. 7.
4. Ibid.
5. Ibid., p. 6.
6. Ibid., p. 7.

inerrant to speak of the Bible. The inerrancy of which he speaks is not in the words, but in the truth of the Bible. He says:

> [The Bible is] inerrant as the only completely authentic witness to God's self-revelation in Christ and his salvation through Christ; inerrant because its truth is the perfect instrument of the Spirit to bring men to faith and righteousness and hope; and inerrant because its teaching, interpreted by the life and work of Christ, is the infallible guide as to how the people of God ought to live and what they can surely believe under the leading of the Spirit of Christ.[7]

Allen honestly recognizes that his view is not without problems and states further:

> The problems are resolved by reverent faith in the Lord of the Scriptures and in the Scriptures themselves as the Word of God, in wholeness and unity in Christ. They are resolved by openmindedness to truth and the fruit of objective research. And they are further resolved by submission to the Holy Spirit who interprets the Word of God in Christ to all persons who desire to know the mind of Christ and to do the will of the Lord.[8]

In summary, Allen has said:

1. The truth of the Bible is inspired but not the words.
2. There is, therefore, the possibility and probability of error in the Bible in wording, fact, and substance.

---

7. Ibid.
8. Ibid., p. 8.

3. The Bible is still an inerrant book—inerrant in the truth it contains.
4. Any problems this view might give can be resolved by submission to the Holy Spirit and by faith in the Lord of Scripture, and in Scripture itself as the Word of God.

Critique

The preceding statements may sound orthodox, impressive, and convincing to some who are trying to understand the theological battle concerning the nature of Scripture. However, I must raise several objections.

First, is there not some relationship between the truth of Scripture and the words that bear it? This is not to advocate that any of our versions or even copies of manuscripts is inerrant. That term must be reserved for the originals. But if we do not have the originals, one might object, are we any better off than the evangelicals who deny inerrancy? Are not we, as well as they, lacking an inerrant text, and therefore are we not seeking to find the inerrant truth through errant words? Why such a concern about inerrant originals that we do not possess anyway?

The answer must be that we are in a better position to know the truth of the Bible if in our textual criticism (that is, search for the original text) we know that the originals were inerrant. In that case, we would seek to determine the inerrant original as closely as possible from the manuscripts and tools at our disposal, and then we would work exegetically (by explaining and critically interpreting) to know the truth revealed in that text. On the other hand, if we deny that the originals were inerrant, we would work textually to determine the original text as nearly as possible. But the difference would be that even when our textual work was finished, and even if we were able to construct the original in perfection (which is not possible), we would be coming to an uncertain original because of its lack of inerrancy. And even if we were to do our exegetical work to perfection, we still would not be sure we had arrived at the truth, because we would be working with uncertain (and how uncertain we would not be able even to guess) manuscripts. Textual criticism and exegesis are difficult enough when they are anchored to the knowledge that the originals were inerrant. The task becomes impossible when that anchor is raised. The point is that there is a relationship between the truth and the inerrant text. Without an inerrant text the truth becomes quite subjective. The matter might be illustrated as follows:

Inerrancy	**Errancy**
1. Interpreter faces manuscripts.	1. Interpreter faces manuscripts.
2. Textual criticism seeks to construct inerrant originals as closely as possible. End result is quite close.	2. Textual criticism seeks to construct errant originals as closely as possible. End result is close, but errant originals still leave many questions as to which parts are true and which are not.
3. Exegesis—applying the principles of hermeneutics (interpretation) to a trustworthy text.	

Inerrancy	Errancy
4. Results—orthodox Christian doctrine, including the person and work of Christ, clearly seen and established as certain.	3. Exegesis—applying the principles of hermeneutics to an uncertain text. Seeking to determine which parts of text are true and which parts are in error always must be part of the work.
	4. Results—not necessarily orthodox Christian doctrine. No certainty one has found the truth. Many different views of the person and work of Christ a possibility.

Could it be that many modern evangelicals who advocate errancy while still standing for the other doctrines of orthodox Christianity, arrived at those other orthodox doctrines before they abandoned inerrancy? There must be a connection between the truth and the accuracy of the words that bear it.

Furthermore, after one has done the textual work, how does he determine which words are the errant ones that Allen admits are present? Is it that some words are fully accurate whereas others are completely in error? Or is it that some words are fully accurate whereas others are partially in error? Or is it that all words are errant in some measure? Could one word be forty percent truthful and another eighty percent accurate? Who determines which words are truthful and which are not? Who determines what degree of a word is accurate? If it seems this is bordering on the ridiculous, so be it. The ridiculousness is not that of inerrancy's position but that of errancy's.

Second, this problem of inerrant truth through errant words cannot be resolved by an existential flight from reality and objectivity, which naively extolls faith in the Holy Spirit, Christ, or Scripture itself, as Allen seeks to do. He calls for an open-mindedness to the fruits of objective research, but when those fruits would lead to difficulties, he exits through the door of existential fuzziness. That door is his only way to avoid the ultimate ridiculousness of errancy's position. If he is left with a Bible containing errors, where else can he go except into the subjective realm?

Allen's problem is as follows. When he rejects the inerrancy of biblical words, how can he then talk about faith in the Holy Spirit, Christ, or Scripture? Is the Christ of history the Christ of Scripture, or is He some uncertain person whom we meet in the existential realm? Allen's dynamic view of the Bible does not guarantee the truth of any aspect of Christ's person and work. For example, on the basis of the dynamic view one cannot insist that Jesus is God, because those words in Scripture that tell us He is God just might be in error, entirely or in part. If the words are not entirely correct, how can one know their meaning? Can they teach deity if one is not sure of their full accuracy or has no way of determining their portion of accuracy? Could not different men conclude that those words have different degrees of accuracy and therefore that they teach different views of Christ? What does *atonement* mean if it is not an accurate word to describe what Christ did for us? What does *resurrection* mean? Could it not be maintained that *resurrection* contains truth or gives us truth, but that it is not an inerrant word, which therefore must be interpreted accordingly?

The argument I am pressing is that there is no Christ of Scripture without an inerrant Word of God. If the words of Scripture are errant and do not give an accurate understanding of His person and work, then one is helplessly confined to uncertainty and confusion regarding who He was and what He did. No flight into a subjective closet of experience can help. Faith is not a leap in the dark over the ruins of an errant Bible, a leap which restores the authority of the Bible and the truth of Christ's person and work. Rather, faith is the casting of oneself upon the objective and certain truth of God as revealed in a trustworthy Word of God.

The dynamic view gives us no certain Word of God. It urges faith in the truth of a Bible containing errors. It urges faith in a Christ of experience who has no certain historical ground. It urges faith in a Holy Spirit who must dynamically mediate the truth from an errant book. How are we certain there even is a Holy Spirit, let alone that He is God, unless He too is revealed in an inerrant Word of God? The words *Christ, Holy Spirit,* and many other precious words of Christianity are meaningless apart from an inerrant Scripture. There can be no inerrant truth apart from an anchor to the inerrant words of Scripture.

4

Where Are the Original Manuscripts?

It has often been stated that the biblical books were inerrant in their original manuscripts. Recently this assertion has raised the same question on several occasions: How can one argue for the inerrancy of originals that do not now exist? This question has been raised in some instances as an honest question, whereas at other times it has been asked by someone who has already answered it negatively.

It matters not who raises that point or with what spirit it is put forth. We must acknowledge it as a serious question and answer it. Why have so many persons down through the years been so confident in the reliability of the original manuscripts, even though no one has ever seen those originals?

How can one today be sure of the trustworthiness of the original manuscripts when neither he nor anyone else in the world has possession of them? Does not common sense preclude that one cannot make a judgment concerning that which he does not possess or that which does not exist? Is it not a prerequisite that one examine the originals to determine their nature and character before one makes statements about the originals' inerrancy?

The problem here is the failure to distinguish between *total evidence* and *sufficient evidence,* and between the uses made of each. The demand for the original manuscripts before one can commit himself to inerrancy is a demand for total evidence. It must be admitted that such evidence for inerrancy is not to be found. Scholars differ regarding how close our manuscript copies approach the originals in respect to dates and complete accuracy; yet, no competent scholar would argue that anyone possesses the originals or that anyone has reconstructed the original text with one hundred percent equality. However, there is a reliable text that for all practical purposes serves us well in study and the formulation of doctrine, even though there is no minutely exact original text. Slight variations in the thousands of manuscripts keeps us from such exactness. Thus I readily admit that we do not possess total evidence upon which to base a case for inerrancy.

That fact need not be troubling, because there

is no total evidence for any of our other doctrinal commitments. For example, we do not possess total evidence for the existence of God. Such would demand that we be able to see God, in order to examine His character and nature. But God is spirit, and this fact negates any possibility of total evidence for His existence. Yet, we still believe in God. As Christians, we have a life and death commitment to Him even though we do not have total evidence of His existence. Our hearts break for the atheist or agnostic who demands total evidence before he acknowledges the existence of God.

However, if we do not believe in the existence of God on the basis of total evidence, is our confidence in Him just a matter of blind faith? Not at all! Faith is certainly a strong factor in our commitment, but we can also point to evidence that is *sufficient* to convince us of God's existence. Although we have never seen Him in His spirit form, and although we have not empirically examined Him in His nature and character, we still believe in God's existence on the basis of other evidence in our world.

Although the evidence around man is sufficient to convince him of God's existence, there is another aspect of sufficient evidence that one must consult in order to understand His nature and character. As Christians, we are committed to accept Scripture as authoritative, sufficient evidence concerning the nature, character, and attributes of God. No one can do otherwise and claim to be a Christian.

We do not have total evidence for any doctrinal truth. Where is total evidence for the Trinity? Our knowledge and commitment to the doctrine of the Trinity is based on sufficient evidence of Scripture. Where is total evidence for the doctrine of creation? Or of the incarnation? Or of the death of Christ? Or of the resurrection? Or of miracles? Total evidence would demand that we be able to examine all those on a firsthand basis. We cannot. Yet, as with the Trinity, we accept those doctrines on the basis of sufficient evidence in Scripture.

My argument concerning the problem of the original manuscripts is that, because we accept sufficient rather than total evidence for our other doctrinal beliefs, it is only proper for us also to accept the sufficient evidence of the Word of God concerning its own nature and character. It is inconsistent to waive the necessity of total evidence concerning all other doctrinal matters and then to turn around and demand total evidence concerning the nature of Scripture itself. If we deny the ability of Scripture to speak authoritatively concerning its own nature, then we also must question its ability to speak authoritatively concerning all other matters of doctrine.

Therefore, the question is not, Do we possess the original manuscripts? but, What does Scripture say about itself?

5

What Is Neo-Orthodoxy?

Among evangelicals today, the term *neo-orthodoxy* has emerged as the negative byword of the hour. That word, whatever it means, is billed as the newest expression of a long line of subversive dangers that have threatened fundamental Christianity. Neo-orthodoxy is said to have invaded churches, denominations, Christian colleges, seminaries, Christian publishing houses, and other established Christian institutions. Some say that its entrance into such Christian institutions often has been so subtle that many laymen and pastors have been unaware of its presence or the damage it can do over an extended period of time. Others would argue on behalf of neo-orthodoxy and assert that it is really a return to orthodoxy from the liberalism of the past. They claim it to be a return to Scripture, revelation and inspiration, the centrality of Christ, and the reality of sin and salvation.

Yet, in spite of all the talk about neo-orthodoxy, whether it be in fear or favor, many persons could not define neo-orthodoxy if asked to do so. For the great multitude of pastors and laymen alike, there is the obvious need for a simple yet distinct definition of neo-orthodoxy. For persons trained in theology, an abundance of works have been written on the subject. Few have explained neo-orthodoxy so that the untrained pastor or bewildered layman could understand the subject. This brief essay is offered with that purpose in mind.

THE FOUNDATIONS OF LIBERALISM

Because neo-orthodoxy is a reaction movement against liberalism, it will be helpful to understand liberalism and its foundations. The story begins with the Enlightenment philosopher Immanuel Kant. In the minds of many philosophers and theologians, he has successfully limited the extent of man's knowledge to the phenomenal realm, that is, to the realm of man's preceptions. Kant reconstructed religion on the basis of man's inner sense of duty, what he called man's categorical imperative. Kant's understanding and argument downgraded the importance of doctrine and elevated man's inner sense of duty.

Friedrich Schleiermacher, influenced by a pietistic Moravian background and by Kant, found what he thought was a new beginning for theology. He placed the supreme theological importance upon man's inner consciousness, his feeling of the divine, or his direct experience with God. That attitude made doctrine the product of the inner experience rather than the experience being founded on true doctrine. By minimizing doctrine Schleiermacher was seeking to reconcile the many religious skeptics who had tired of the innumerable doctrinal controversies of Christianity. Doctrine was only the shell, according to Schleiermacher, while the real kernel was the feeling, the experience, and the emotion one had as he possessed the direct consciousness of the divine. Both Kant and Schleiermacher, therefore, attacked the foundation of Christianity—doctrine and truth contained in a biblical revelation.

Along with those two ideas, there came another movement in the late nineteenth century. It was known as higher criticism. That method of analysis sought to apply to the Bible the same principles of literary criticism that one would apply to any other book. For each book of the Bible it asked probing questions about origin, authorship, inspiration, historical accuracy, geographical correctness, and scientific implications. At each of those points grave doubts surfaced concerning the truthfulness of Scripture. Without going into detail, for purposes of this essay, it can be said that higher criticism concluded the Bible to be a book of legends, myths, and errors (of history, geography, and science).

Subsequently, more doubt arose about the Bible. The new concepts and opinions of science flexed their muscles of authority. The most important of those supposedly positive concepts was Darwin's theory of evolution. It raised further doubt concerning the biblical account of creation, the origin and development of man, man's present state, and his future. Darwin's theories added weight to the already growing doubts about the biblical doctrines, which doubts had been raised by higher criticism's handling of Genesis.

The influence of that total context of doubt was extremely detrimental to the authority and reliability of Scripture. How could anyone take a book containing so many errors as his authority in religious matters? As a result of that destructive work on the Bible, liberalism concluded that Christ was not the incarnate Son of God, born of a virgin. Neither was He resurrected to glory following His death. Man was not a fallen creature who was in need of divine regeneration. Rather he was the evolving being who had sprung to life millennia ago in some primeval ooze. And man was now scaling the ladder of evolution to perfection and supreme glory. Further, liberalism was convinced that doctrine was not important and that man's utmost efforts must be aimed in the direction of humanitarian acts.

The Liberal-Fundamentalist Battle

After the turn of the century, liberalism spread quickly throughout the United States, although it had originated in Europe. There developed in this nation what came to be known as the liberal-fundamentalist battle. The fundamentalists were committed to a divinely-inspired and inerrant Bible, as opposed to liberalism's book of errors. The fundamentalists exalted the divine, virgin-born, crucified and resurrected Savior, as opposed to liberalism's merely human Jesus of example. Fundamentalists heralded that the human race was fallen and totally corrupt in sin and in need of regeneration, as opposed to liberalism's evolving man on the threshhold of perfection and utmost glory. The lines were clearly drawn and the battle raged, with the fundamentalists standing courageously, if not always wisely and intelligently.

The Entrance of Karl Barth

In the early 1920s a young theologian named Karl Barth came to the battlefront. The son of a liberal theology professor and reared in the liberal position, Barth went forth to preach and pastor. Much to his dismay and surprise he discovered that his liberalism provided nothing to preach. He was convinced that a return to Scripture was the answer to his problem. But that conviction produced a terrible dilemma. He was convinced that he could not remain a liberal, but he was equally persuaded that he could not move completely into fundamentalism. His education in liberalism had done its destructive work—the Bible was a book of errors that could not be verbally inspired.

How did Barth solve that dilemma? One should note carefully his solution, because the next step seems to be an impossible move, but Barth took it and it has been taken by scores of others since. He solved his problem by removing revelation from the Bible text itself and placing it into the experience of the biblical writers. That is to say, Barth was convinced that the biblical writers had revelational experiences with God. However, when the biblical writers wrote about their revelational experiences with God, they did not pen propositional and revelational truth, because God is so transcendent and so "Wholly Other" that neither He nor His truth can be confined to human words. Rather, the writers simply gave human accounts of their revelational experiences. Thus, according to Barth, the Bible text was the erring human witness of revelation and not revelation itself. Therefore, one need not be surprised to find in that human account of the revelational experience all kinds of errors—geographical, historical, and scientific.

At this point one might properly ask how Barth's view of Scripture gave him any better Bible to preach than the one possessed by the liberals. Barth would have answered that by saying that in the preaching of the Bible, even as a book with errors, the divine revelational encounter could repeat itself in the life of the one the Bible addresses. By that means the Bible "becomes" the Word of God today as the Holy Spirit brings it alive.

CONCLUSION

Barth's view was called neo-orthodoxy because it was believed he had moved back toward orthodoxy. Actually he had stopped at a halfway point between orthodoxy and liberalism. His position just as easily could have been called neoliberalism, which might have been a better name for it.

One of the key problems with Barth's view of the Bible is in the realm of authority. How can a Bible full of errors ever produce any objective truth? How can a Bible, which must be interpreted subjectively, ever grant a solid authority for our churches? How can it ever give even one definite and positive "thus saith the Lord." Each interpreter becomes his own authority and relies on his experience, thus making it impossible to know when he or any other person has apprehended the truth. My experience with Scripture may disagree with Barth's experience. What then? Who shall be our human authority in this realm of subjective exegesis?

The element that makes neo-orthodoxy so dangerous is that it uses the words of orthodoxy, but reinterprets them according to its own definition and purpose. Unlike liberalism, it does lay great stress on inspiration and revelation, but it does not hold to verbal inspiration *and* equate the Bible with revelation. Neo-orthodoxy does speak often of the centrality of Christ, but it does not hold to the orthodox person and work of Christ. Concerning salvation, Barth's exegesis results in a universal salvation through the elected Jesus Christ, who was also the elector. This is a clear example of Barth's subjective interpretation, which restates Scripture to mean whatever he wants and uses portions of Scripture out of context.

Not all neo-orthodox theologians agree with Barth on the preceding points. However, because of a similar view of revelation and a refusal to return to verbal inspiration, the approach to Scripture is in line with Barth's subjective analysis. Some theologians have sought to correct what they believed were Barth's errors, and in the process they have moved even closer to orthodoxy. Others, even those in the evangelical camp, have been influenced by Barth, because they are seeking to argue for inerrant truth in an errant Scripture. There exists a scholarly hesitation to take one's stand with the doctrine of verbal inspiration. Men continue to build upon and be influenced by the structures of liberalism and Barth. Theologies are given new names and cherished, meaningful terms are redefined, but modern theology will not escape the liberal and Barthian influence until it returns to the inerrancy of Scripture.

6

Evangelical Double-Talk Concerning Scripture

How are we to judge the nature of Scripture? For many years Christians have allowed the Bible to speak for itself concerning its nature, just as they have allowed it to speak with authority on all other doctrinal subjects. When Jesus said that Scripture could not be broken (John 10:35), that settled the matter. When Paul stated that all Scripture is given by inspiration of God (2 Timothy 3:16), that carried great weight also. Great importance was attached to systematizing the biblical witness concerning its own nature, even as importance was given to the scriptural witness in every other area of doctrine. Scripture was the final word on every doctrine, including the doctrine of Scripture.

But now some modern evangelicals are saying that we have been going about it all wrong. Instead of allowing Scripture to speak, we ought to be allowing the phenomena of Scripture to speak to us about what kind of book it is. In a lead article in a 1974 publication, Bernard Ramm rejects the first method (Scripture speaks for itself) while he argues for the second (the phenomena must be allowed to speak).[1] Concerning the first method he says:

> The customary one is to read the Scriptures and pick out texts which refer to inspiration or revelation or the word of God and from these texts construe one's theology of Scripture. This has been the method of such stalwarts of this traditon as Lee, Warfield, and Gaussen. In their opinion Scripture being what it is must be verbally inspired, plenarily inspired, and inerrant in all matters of faith and fact.[2]

Concerning the second method Ramm says:

> The second approach is to first grasp the character of Scripture as it stands before us. . . . Viewed from Genesis to Revelation what is Scripture like in fine and in large? What is the phenomenology (i.e., careful accurate description) of Scripture? Only by a phenomenological examination of

---

1. Bernard Ramm, "Scripture As A Theological Content," *Review and Expositor* 71 (Spring 1974): 149-61.
2. Ibid., pp. 149-50.

> Scripture which details out the phenomena of Scripture may we adequately state the theological attributes of Scripture.[3]

The careful, accurate description of Scripture (phenomena) that Ramm gives consists of four points.[4]

1. *Scripture is history, a very special kind of history.* It is different from secular history in that its events have great theological importance concerning the past and future.
2. *Scripture is literature.* That is to say, Scripture uses all kinds of literary methods and types. Failure to recognize that could result in serious errors of interpretation.
3. *Scripture is a revelation to man as man, and to man in his own culture.* Scripture comes to man in his language and in a specific cultural setting.
4. *Scripture is a partial revelation.* It tells man something about God, man, Christ, and so forth, but not about all things. It is sufficient but not exhaustive.

Ramm closes his statement about the phenomena of Scripture by saying:

> The phenomenological treatment of Scripture prevents us from overstating the nature of Scripture. Whatever attributes we may assign to Scripture as it functions theologically or authoritatively in the church must be within the context of the specific characteristics of Scripture.[5]

3. Ibid., p. 150.
4. Ibid., pp. 150-53.
5. Ibid., p. 153.

To summarize Ramm's statements so far, one should note his following points. First, the nature of Scripture cannot be determined by a consideration of what Scripture says about itself. Second, the nature of Scripture must be determined by examining the phenomena of Scripture, that is, by carefully examining Scripture as it stands before us, in order to note its clear characteristics. Third, such an examination shows that Scripture is an unusual kind of history, has various kinds of literature, is the revelation of God to man in his specific culture, and is the sufficient revelation of God to man (even though not exhaustive, it is sufficient to meet man's need).

From that basis Ramm sets forth the theological attributes of Scripture. He says in summary:

1. *The Scripture is the Word of God, but not in any infallible or inerrant sense regarding the wording.* Having already stated that Scripture is culturally, historically, and linguistically conditioned, Ramm has excluded an orthodox view of verbal inspiration. Still, however, he believes the Bible has theological integrity. It may in some theological sense be called the Word of God.
2. *The Scripture is the revelation of God, but again not infallible or inerrant.* Scripture is a revelation from God, but it wears the garments of ancient cultures. God reveals Himself in a variety of ways, but not necessarily in any "author-scribe" manner. Revelation is more than the

best that man has to offer, but it is less than inerrant.

3. *Scripture is the inspired Word of God, but not in any high sense that would guarantee infallibility and inerrancy.* Ramm would not wish to eliminate the doctrine of inspiration as a category of theological discussion, but he admits he is uneasy about such words as infallible and inerrant. Too many problems arise when one seeks to put Scripture into that mold, he believes.
4. *Scripture is the canonical Word of God, but the limits of the canon are still open.* This means that the sixty-six books in our Bible are recognized as the Word of God, but that other books still could be added to it.
5. *Canonical Scripture is the authoritative Word of God in the church.* God is the supreme authority in theology and Scripture reflects that supreme authority to a degree—as it reflects correctly the mind of God. This viewpoint causes Scripture to fall short of the truth of God in word and letter. God's Word cannot be reduced in exact quality to a book. But the Scripture is still the authoritative Word of God, and has the power to become the Word of God over and over again.
6. *Scripture is doctrinal.* It is the propositional Word of God, but again not in any high sense.[6]

---

6. Ibid., pp. 154-61.

Comments and Critique

It has been necessary to give a rather lengthy presentation of Ramm's view, but such a presentation should better enable me to comment upon his position.

First, Ramm's position is a supreme example of the evangelical double-talk that is going on concerning the nature of Scripture. High sounding statements, using traditional evangelical language, are made about Scripture. But then the meaning of that language is undermined by further statements and observations. Scripture is the Word of God—but not fully. Scripture is the revelation of God—but not infallible and inerrant. Scripture is the inspired Word of God—but not in the highest sense. Scripture is the canonical Word of God—but the canon is potentially still open. Scripture is the authoritative Word of God—but it only reflects the mind of God in some measure or to some degree. Scripture is the doctrinal Word of God—but only potentially. Such use of evangelical language enables modern evangelicals who do not hold to inerrancy still to answer "yes" to probing questions concerning the nature of Scripture.

Second, Ramm is inconsistent to reject Scripture's ability to speak for itself by its texts and passages concerning its nature, but then to allow the phenomena to speak. He says the first method is an a priori method, but indicates the second is not a priori and does not have presuppositions.[7]

7. Ibid., p. 150.

Ramm, however, cannot escape presuppositions. He presupposes that the phenomena of Scripture can speak authoritatively and correctly. He spends no time in showing the validity and trustworthiness of the phenomena, but assumes their credibility and builds his argument thereupon. Further, after examining the phenomena he assumes that his conclusions are correct, even though others have examined the same phenomena and have come to entirely different conclusions. An example of such faulty reasoning would be Ramm's conclusion that the Bible is a special kind of history because its events have special theological significance. Such a conclusion is a hopeful one, but it is not conclusive. The only basis for asserting that Scripture contains a special kind of history is not by a mere examination of the scriptural stories, but by a realization that the Bible, by its own testimony, claims to be a special kind of book in history and every other realm.

Ramm is also inconsistent when he concludes that an examination of scriptural phenomena can show that Scripture is the revelation of God. Since he has excluded the possibility of Scripture's being able to speak with authority concerning itself, on what ground does he claim it to be the revelation of God? Others have examined the same phenomena and have come to opposite conclusions. If the scriptural wording is questionable and cannot speak with authority, why should the phenomena be so trustworthy to prove that

Scripture is the revelation of God? Is there not some relation between the wording and the phenomena? Can errant wording grant us trustworthy phenomena to examine?

In conclusion, Ramm is guilty of double-talk in two respects. First, he errs in his use of dual language. He attempts to use all the traditional evangelical wording, but in such a way that he negates and softens much of its proper meaning. Second, he errs when he seeks to convince us that his position regarding the phenomena has no presuppositions and that it is more capable of establishing the nature of Scripture than is Scripture's own testimony.

7

Luther: Errancy or Inerrancy?

As the battle over the nature of the Bible intensifies, a strange development is rising through the smoke of debate. Both sides of the issue, errancy and inerrancy, are claiming to represent Luther and Calvin. Such conflicting claims raise the question, Were Luther and Calvin so unclear in their writings that both sides can honestly use them in debate, or are the Reformers being prostituted so that modern theological viewpoints can gain acceptance and respectability? This essay will deal with that question as it relates to Luther.

In a recent publication, Jack Rogers seeks to place Luther in the camp of errancy. After a brief discussion of Luther, which includes a few quotations, Rogers says, concerning Luther's view of Scripture:

> Luther's concept of biblical authority followed from his personal relationship to the Bible. For him, Christ alone was without error and was the essential Word of God. Thus, Luther's faith was in the subject matter of Scripture, not its form, which was the object of scholarly investigation. When Luther said of Scripture, "There is no falsehood in it," he was speaking not about technical accuracy, but the ability of the Word to accomplish righteousness in us.[1]

Rogers follows this with a quotation in which Luther does say there is no falsehood in the doctrine of Christ. But the question is, Has Rogers shown that Luther did not believe in the inerrancy of Scripture? Does his argumentation prior to his above-quoted conclusion support what that conclusion says? Does his quotation from Luther support that conclusion? Has he considered other data that might be pertinent to the discussion?

I am convinced that Roger's argument is faulty on several counts.

---

1. Jack Rogers, "The Church Doctrine of Biblical Authority," in *Biblical Authority,* ed. Jack Rogers (Waco, Texas: Word, 1977), p. 25. This essay does not deal just with Luther's concept of Scripture. Rather, the author attempts to show a philosophical relation and development of the two current views of the nature of Scripture among evangelicals. Even though this is Roger's main thrust, it still must be pointed out that he fails to show that the Reformers denied inerrancy, and he ignores some of their key statements that indicate they held to inerrancy.

First, his argumentation and quotations prior to his conclusion do not support that conclusion. His conclusion is that Luther held to inerrancy of subject matter in the Bible, but not inerrancy of technical matter. What are the arguments and discussion that precede his conclusion? They may be summarized as follows:

1. Luther had no confidence in human reason in the area of spiritual matters.
2. The purpose of Scripture, according to Luther, is to speak to us of salvation.
3. Scripture comes to us, according to Luther, with no external glory (which Rogers for some reason calls an imperfect form).
4. It is only by the power of the Spirit that we come to place our faith in the Word of God, according to Luther.[2]

At that point Rogers draws his conclusion that Luther did not hold to inerrancy. However, Luther's lack of confidence in human reason says nothing about errant Scripture. Luther's conviction that the purpose of Scripture is to speak about salvation is not a supporting premise for errancy either. Nor does Luther's statement about Scripture coming to us with no external glory support errancy, unless one incorrectly defines that statement to mean an errant form, which Rogers does. Christ also came to us with no external

---

2. Ibid., pp. 24-25.

glory, but certainly not in an errant manner. Rogers grossly misinterprets Luther on that point. Luther's final conviction that the power of the Spirit is necessary for faith in the Word of God also fails to support his conclusion.

Roger's final quotation from Luther (page 25 in Roger's book) does accurately register Luther as stating that there is no falsehood in the doctrine of Christ's righteousness for us, but that is a far cry from a denial of inerrancy. Those who hold to the doctrine of inerrancy would also adamantly declare that there is no falsehood in the doctrine of Christ's righeousness for us. In fact, I would press the point that the reason one can be positive of the work and righteousness of Christ for us is because of the reality of inerrant Scripture.

Roger's failure in the presentation of his case does not end merely with faulty argumentation and bad logic. He further fails to consider the many passages in which Luther indicates a belief in inerrancy. A. Skevington Wood, in a book devoted entirely to Luther and Scripture, gives one whole chapter to Luther's view of inspiration.[3] Some of the phrases of Luther in reference to Scripture are as follows: "honour the Holy Spirit by believing his Words and accepting them as the

---

3. A Skevington Wood, *Captive to the Word: Martin Luther: Doctor of Sacred Scripture* (Grand Rapids: Eerdmans, 1969), pp. 139-48.

divine truth";[4] "inspiration extends to 'phraseology and diction' ";[5] "spoken by the Holy Spirit";[6] "the prophets are those 'into whose mouth the Holy Spirit has given the words' ";[7] "the Scriptures have never erred";[8] "the Scriptures cannot lie";[9] "the perfectly clear, certain, sure words of God, which can never deceive us or allow us to err";[10] "prize a single tittle and letter more highly than the whole world."[11]

Usually references of that nature in Luther's writings have been overlooked, ignored, or quickly swept aside in light of Luther's overall definition of the Word of God. For Luther the phrase *Word of God* had a wide usage. He used it to refer to the Bible, the word of absolution, the word of promise, the gospel, and even the oral word or sermon. The Word of God to him was something

---

4. Martin Luther, *Luther's Works,* ed. Jaroslav J. Pelikan and Helmut T. Lehmann, 55 vols. (Philadelphia and St. Louis, 1955-), 22:10. (Also in Wood, pp. 141-42.)
5. Luther, *Works,* 22:119. (Also in Wood, p. 143.)
6. Martin Luther, *D. Martin Luthers sämtliche Schriften,* ed. Johann Georg Walch, 24 vols. Revised. (St. Louis, 1880-1910), 3:1895. (Also in Wood, p. 141.)
7. Martin Luther, *D. Martin Luthers Werke, kritische Gesamtausgabe,* ed. J. F. K. Knaake et al, 57 vols. (Weimer, 1883-), 3:172. (Also in Wood, p. 142.)
8. Luther, *Works,* 32:11. (Also in Wood, p. 144.)
9. Luther, *Works,* 27:258. (Also in Wood, p. 144.)
10. Luther, *Works,* 47:308. (Also in Wood, p. 145.)
11. Luther, *Works,* 37:308. (Also in Wood, p. 145.)

dynamic. But the Bible was the Word of God in a unique sense, as can be seen from the above-quoted references to it. The dynamic working of the Word of God in promise, absolution, gospel, and even word and sermon was dependent upon Scripture, which contained no deception—not even in one word.

Again, Luther's references to inspiration and inerrancy often have been discarded because he gave evidence of being critical of Scripture, particularly some books and details. One ought to remind himself, however, that Luther made no claim for the inerrancy of the manuscripts possessed in his day, but of the originals. His labors as a textual critic were attempts to determine the original text. One also must remember Luther's historical situation. In many areas of the Christian faith he was seeking to sort out what was truly of God from what was only Roman Catholic tradition. If in the process he raised some jarring questions, one must remember the context from which he spoke and his ever clear adherence to an inerrant Scripture. One must not take statements that reflect Luther's struggles and interpret them to say that he denied inerrancy.

Many modern readers are reading Luther in light of the twentieth-century inerrancy debate. Before they will acknowledge that Luther held to inerrancy, they demand that he speak in the categories of that debate. If such a demand be pressed upon past theologians then it would have to be concluded that even the doctrinal statements of the leading denominations and theological schools of the first fifty years of this century did not hold to inerrancy. However, it is beyond dispute that those institutions did. The point is that the categories of thought and definition have changed because of the influx of neo-orthodoxy, which change has required a restatement and redefinition of the inerrancy position in order to provide more clarity now. Such clarity was not needed in Luther's day because the inerrancy of Scripture was not the issue. Even so, Luther spoke with a clarity that comes through to us if we read him in his historical setting and consider all his statements regarding the nature of the Bible. He clearly subscribed to an inerrant Scripture.

8

Calvin: Errancy or Inerrancy?

As Martin Luther is being claimed by both camps of evangelicals in the battle for the Bible, so is John Calvin. In the same essay as the one mentioned in chapter 7, Jack Rogers presents a case that seeks to put Calvin in the camp of errancy. Rogers analyzes Calvin's view of Scripture and makes the following points:

1. All men have an innate knowledge of God.
2. The innate knowledge of God is suppressed by sinful human beings leaving them responsible for their condition.
3. Because the suppression of innate knowledge blurs man's knowledge of God, God gave another and better help to direct man to God. That better revelation is the Word which brings

us a knowledge of salvation through the Scriptures.

4. Only the internal testimony of the Holy Spirit can persuade one that God is the author of the Scriptures.
5. The central theme of the Scriptures is Jesus Christ and the purpose of the Scriptures is that we might know Christ in a saving way.
6. God represents Himself to us not as he is in Himself, but as He seems to us.
7. The saving message of the Bible could come through the imperfect form of words.
8. The teaching of the Bible does not have to be harmonized with science.[1]

Rogers correctly estimates Calvin's view of Scripture. The agreement with Rogers's presentation, however, does not mean that I agree with his conclusion that Calvin believed in an errant Scripture. None of the first five points would grant any proof that would place Calvin in the camp of errancy. The strongest ammunition in Rogers's arsenal that might convict Calvin of errancy would be the last three points. Those points need individual analysis to determine whether or not they support Rogers's contention.

God Represents Himself to Us as He Seems

What about the claim that God represents Him-

---

1. Jack Rogers, "The Church Doctrine of Biblical Authority," in *Biblical Authority,* ed. Jack Rogers (Waco, Texas: Word, 1977), pp. 25-29.

self to us as He seems, not as He is? First, one must ask if that is what Calvin believed. The answer is yes, according to his own testimony. For example, in commenting on the expression that attributes repentance to God, Calvin said:

> What then is meant by the term repentance? The very same that is meant by other forms of expression, by which God is described to us humanly. Because our weakness cannot reach his height, any description which we receive of him must be lowered to our capacity in order to be intelligible. And the mode of lowering is to represent him not as he really is, but as we conceive of him.[2]

Second, one must ask if such a conviction places Calvin in the camp of errancy. The answer is no. He was simply acknowledging that the Bible uses human language to describe nonhuman things (anthropomorphisms) and other modes of speech to communicate the truth of God to man. The claim made by inerrancy is for a perfection of the words that the original manuscripts used to convey the knowledge of God to man's level of understanding. A perfection of words to describe God in inexhaustible exactness at every point is not claimed, but Rogers seems to have confused the two possible claims.

The Saving Message through Imperfect Words

Concerning the seventh point that the message

---

2. John Calvin, *The Institutes of the Christian Religion,* trans. Henry Beveridge, 2 vols. (Grand Rapids: Eerdmans, 1964), 1:195.

of the Bible may come through imperfect words, Rogers again states Calvin correctly. The reference cited at that juncture is in relation to the apostles' manner of quoting Old Testament Scripture. It reads:

> They [the apostles] were not over-scrupulous in quoting words provided that they did not misuse Scripture for their convenience. We must always look at the purpose for which quotations are made . . . but as far as the words are concerned, as in other things which are not relevant to the present purpose, they allow themselves some indulgence.[3]

Rogers's assumption appears to be that since Calvin recognized that the apostles were not meticulous in the exact quotation of scriptural passages, therefore he did not hold to the importance and inerrancy of words but rather to the importance and infallibility of the truth. That is an improper assumption. All who hold to inerrancy would admit that the truth must at some point come to us through fallible means. Christians preach and teach the truth in their own human words, which are fallible. We state the truth from a passage of Scripture or even quote Scripture in a general way. This in no way commits one to an errant Scripture. If one believed that at every point only perfect words would convey truth, one could

3. John Calvin, *Hebrews and the First and Second Epistles of Peter,* trans. William B. Johnston, ed. D. W. and T. F. Torrance (Grand Rapids: Eerdmans, 1963), p. 136. (Also in Rogers, p. 28)

not preach or witness in any manner except to quote Scripture from its original manuscripts (which we do not possess). When one, with Calvin, admits that truth may come to us in imperfect words, he in no wise is indicating that the original manuscripts were also imperfect. Therefore, the fact of the biblical writers' quoting Scripture in a general manner does not violate inerrancy.

For Calvin, as for Luther, it is clear that there was faith in an inerrant text, which text stands behind and anchors man's general use of translated Scripture in its imperfect form. If it were not for that anchor, our general use would be adrift. Calvin speaks of such an inerrant text in terms that clearly indicate a commitment to inerrancy.

> But since no daily responses are given from heaven, and the Scriptures are the only records in which God has been pleased to consign his truth to perpetual rememberance, the full authority which they ought to possess with the faithful is not recognised, unless they are believed to have come from heaven, as directly as if God had been heard giving utterance to them.[4]

> Hence, the highest proof of Scripture is uniformly taken from the character of him whose word it is.[5]

> Nay, words uniformly said by the prophets to have been spoken by the Lord of Hosts, are by Christ and his apostles ascribed to the Holy Spirit. Hence

4. Calvin, *Institutes,* 1:68.
5. Ibid., 1:71.

> it follows that the Spirit is the true Jehovah, who dictated the prophecies.[6]

> Although, as I have observed, there is this difference between the apostles and their successors, they were sure and authentic amanuenses of the Holy Spirit; and, therefore, their writings are to be regarded as the oracles of God, whereas others have no other office than to teach what is delivered and sealed in the holy Scriptures.[7]

The Bible and Science

The last point that supposedly places Calvin in the fold of errancy concerns a statement about the Bible and science. He said:

> Moses wrote in popular style things which, without instruction, all ordinary persons, endued with common sense are able to understand; but astronomers investigate with great labour whatever the sagacity of the human mind can comprehend. . . . Nor [is] this science to be condemned. . . . astronomy is not only pleasant, but also very useful to be known. . . . Nor did Moses truly wish to withdraw us from this pursuit. . . . Had he spoken of things generally unknown, the uneducated might have pleaded in excuse that such subjects were beyond their capacity.[8]

---

6. Ibid., 1:123.
7. Ibid., 2:395.
8. John Calvin, *The First Book of Moses Called Genesis,* trans. John King, 2 vols. (Grand Rapids: Eerdmans, 1948), 1:86-87. (Also in Rogers, p. 29)

Does this passage from Calvin place him in the bounds of errancy? Note the following points that Calvin makes and the implications that can be drawn from them.

1. *Moses did not write in scientific language, but in a manner that common men could understand.*

   Calvin was acknowledging that the Bible is not a technical, scientific textbook, but that is not to say that the Bible can be in error concerning scientific matters. He was simply saying that the Bible speaks understandably concerning those matters. Would it be understandable if the Bible spoke in error concerning those matters? The Bible speaks simply but accurately and therefore does not contain scientific errors.

2. *Science investigates a subject in greater detail and minutely defines a subject, all of which is proper and acceptable to a Christian.*

   Calvin was not saying that science is infallible in all its investigations and statements. He did not say that true science and the Bible would disagree. He did not say we are to use the Bible with science as our interpretive tool. He simply recognized that science has a proper place for the Christian as he explores his world. The Bible is still the inerrant Word of God.

The overall conclusion must be that Calvin, like

Luther, cannot be claimed by modern evangelicals who wish to promote their views of an errant Scripture. Not one of the eight points cited by Rogers, nor all of them massed together, can declare that Calvin held to a modern evangelical viewpoint of inerrant truth through errant words. Calvin, on the contrary, was committed to inerrant truth through and because of inerrant words given by the Holy Spirit in the Word of God.

9

Will The Real Jesus Please Stand Up?

For several centuries critical scholars, not satisfied with the Jesus of Scripture, have been seeking to get the "real," historical Jesus to stand up. The search was begun during the Enlightenment. Armed with a naturalistic and rationalistic bias, the scholars sought desperately to end the tension that they thought existed between the Jesus of history and the Christ of faith.

The Search for the Historical Jesus

Hermann Samuel Reimarus

The father of the quest for the historical Jesus is

considered by many to be Hermann Samuel Reimarus (1694-1768). In his *Apology,* a work published anonymously by the philosopher G. E. Lessing after the death of Reimarus, he shocked the religious world and even deterred many young men from the pursuit of the ministry. He argued that the real Jesus of history was completely opposite to the one recorded in Scripture.

According to Reimarus, Jesus, His disciples, and the people of that day expected Him to set up a worldly kingdom. When He was not enthroned following the triumphal entry, He hid; but He was found and taken by the Pharisees and crucified while He cried out that God had forsaken Him. It was following His death that the disciples, from greedy and selfish motives to gain power and worldly advantages, altered completely the person of Jesus. They fabricated stories to make him a savior who had died a sacrificial death and had risen from the dead. Thus Reimarus thought he had unveiled the real Jesus of history.

DAVID FRIEDRICH STRAUSS

Not everyone agreed that Reimarus had finally produced the Jesus of history. Germany was rocked again, this time by the work of a young twenty-seven-year-old scholar named David Friedrich Strauss (1808-74). Armed with the conviction that Matthew, Mark, and Luke (the synoptic gospels) were the only sources to be used in the search, Strauss thought he had produced a synthesis between supernaturalism and naturalism by his mythical view. He argued that much of the life of Jesus was clouded in myth because myth had been the vehicle of writing employed by the disciples. That which the disciples presented was eternal truth in mythical form.

Therefore, the Jesus of the synoptics was far different from the Christ of faith, and the Christ of faith could be seen only as one acknowledged the myth and interpreted it not as fact or history, but as the bearer of eternal truth.

CHRISTIAN HERMANN WEISS

The Jesus of history still eluded the grasp of the scholars, even Strauss. Shortly thereafter, Christian Hermann Weiss (1801-66), feeling Strauss had fractured the connection between the gospels and history, sought to build a life of Jesus on the gospel of Mark. Because of Mark's graphic details Weiss believed it was the earliest gospel and therefore the most trustworthy. He reopened the door for an historical consideration of the person and life of Jesus.

This is not to say that Weiss felt that Mark was an accurate presentation of the life of Jesus. He considered many events in Mark to be historical, but many not to be historical. Therefore he does not even attempt to write a life of Jesus, but gives only a general sketch of gospel history through Mark's main outline. Needless to say, Weiss rejected much of the miraculous and supernatural, including the resurrection. He said the resurrection was a myth that had attached itself to the historical fact of Jesus' spiritual presence with His disciples after His death.

WILLIAM WREDE

The argument for the superiority and priority of Mark did not last very long. William Wrede (1859-1906) agreed that Mark's gospel was the oldest, but he also saw it as a compromising rewrite to unite two different early church viewpoints about Jesus. According to Wrede, Mark pictured Jesus as one holding a secret messiahship before His death (a messiahship known only to the demons and his disciples), and as one holding an open messiahship after the resurrection.

That fabrication and compromise invented by Mark has left modern man with a thoroughly unhistorical and unreliable account of the life of Jesus.

Therefore, in its search for the historical Jesus, scholarship had moved to the point of rejecting all the gospel accounts of His life. The search had started by considering all the gospels. John was rejected first, in favor of the synoptics. Then Matthew and Luke were rejected in favor of Mark. Then Wrede brought in the rejection of Mark. All the historical sources were destroyed, according to the scholars. What possibly could be the next step?

Form Criticism

Since the historical sources had been ruled out by the scholars, a new method was needed. That new method was form criticism. It postulated that there had been a generation between the period of Jesus' ministry and the gospel sources we possess today. Therefore, form criticism said scholars must examine the period of time between the ministry of Christ and the recording of our present gospel sources. During that period, the stories of Jesus circulated, developed, and even changed. As those stories had circulated, they had fallen into certain forms. A skilled scholar, it was thought, could move back behind the written records and get to the originals by means of critical analysis of the forms. That method was very subjective and many different opinions prevailed, again making the search for the real Jesus quite fruitless.

The New Quest

Again the attempt to construct a life of Jesus by the methods of the critical scholars seemed at an end. The rationalistic search of the gospels had failed to unearth Him. The attempt to study the pericopes (sections of the gospels) and disconnected stories could not yield reliable results because of the subjectivity involved. There was a need for a new quest, unless of course the scholars were to throw in the towel and admit their failure. The new quest came through such men as

Gunther Bornkamm and James M. Robinson. Bornkamm said it is a mistake to believe that the gospels were written to fulfill any historical purpose. Faith takes precedence over history—the heart of the gospels is not history, rather the heart is the church's faith. The gospels were directed to the practical use of the believing church to whom history meant very little. More important than the history is the kerygma (the apostolic proclamation of salvation). That is to say, history and truth have little in common. It is not necessary for the kerygma to be historically true, according to Bornkamm.

James M. Robinson followed into this existential realm, also, when he argued that the nineteenth-century scholars failed because of their view of history. History is more than cold, hard facts of names and places. It is living and creative. Robinson argued for the need to center on the kerygma and an encounter with God, not on the historical facts of the gospels. It is not the historical Jesus who is to be sought, but the kerygmatic Jesus of experience. In such an encounter He becomes a real and visible person to us, as real and as visible as if we could find Him in the written gospels.

In this new quest one has once again a fracture between history and the real Jesus. He is not to be found in history, but in experience. It does not matter what history says of Him, one can know Him in certainty by a spiritual encounter today.

CONCLUSION

Those futile quests of the scholars of the past two centuries have been presented for one purpose—to show the great importance of holding firmly to the inspiration and inerrancy of Scripture. When one's confidence in Scripture begins to blur, then so does the historical Jesus, as proved by the critical scholars' views. In turn, when the historical Jesus blurs, so does the only plan of salvation. There is only one way the real person and work of Christ can emerge, rise, and stand, and that is through a divinely-inspired, infallible, and inerrant Word of God. One might just as well sing about "Lucy In the Sky with Diamonds" or "Pink Marmalade," as did some escapists of song, as to search for the historical Jesus and Christ with scholars who reject the inerrancy of Scripture.

That is why the present discussion among evangelicals concerning the nature of Scripture must continue. The nature of Scripture is linked vitally to one's view of the person and work of Christ. Only as evangelicals hold to inerrancy and infallibility can they know that they are preaching the real, historical, and saving Jesus Christ.

Moody Press, a ministry of the Moody Bible Institute, is designed for education, evangelization, and edification. If we may assist you in knowing more about Christ and the Christian life, please write us without obligation: *Moody Press, c/o MLM, Chicago, Illinois 60610.*